MARX & ENGELS

MARX & ENGELS

A biographical introduction

Ernesto Che Guevara

Centro de Estudios
CHE GUEVARA

Ocean Press
Melbourne ▪ New York ▪ London
www.oceanbooks.com.au

Cover design by David Alfonso

ISBN 978-1-920888-92-3
Library of Congress Catalog Card Number 2007942838

First printed 2008
Printed in Mexico

Also published by Ocean Sur in Spanish as
Marx y Engels: Una síntesis biográfica, ISBN 978-1-921235-25-2

PUBLISHED BY OCEAN PRESS

Australia: GPO Box 3279, Melbourne, Victoria 3001, Australia
                Fax: (61-3) 9329 5040 Tel: (61-3) 9326 4280
                E-mail: info@oceanbooks.com.au

USA: 511 Avenue of the Americas, #96
                New York, NY 10011-8436

OCEAN PRESS TRADE DISTRIBUTORS

United States and Canada: **Consortium Book Sales and Distribution**
        Tel: 1-800-283-3572   www.cbsd.com

Australia and New Zealand: **Palgrave Macmillan**
        E-mail: customer.service@macmillan.com.au

UK and Europe: **Turnaround Publisher Services**
        E-mail: orders@turnaround-uk.com

Mexico and Latin America: **Ocean Sur**
        E-mail: info@oceansur.com

ocean

www.oceanbooks.com.au
info@oceanbooks.com.au

Contents

Editors' note   1

Marx & Engels: A biographical
    introduction   13

Notes   75

Che's reading list on Marx and Engels   77

"Many of Che's comments about Marx reveal the link between the biographer and his subject and might also refer to Che himself."

Editors' note

"Now St. Karl is paramount, the axis, as he will be for all the years I remain on the face of the earth..."* So wrote young Ernesto Guevara de la Serna referring to Karl Marx in a letter sent from Mexico to his mother in October 1956, reflecting his passage through a crucial formative stage and foreshadowing his future intense intellectual vocation in which he would seek to explore his surroundings, while his knowledge extended beyond the limits of theory, nourished by the complexity and contradictions of real life. This interrelationship of theory and practice led to an extraordinary revolutionary impulse and to a mission as yet undefined.

---

* Cited by Ernesto Guevara Lynch, *Aquí va un soldado de América*, (Spain: Editorial Plaza y Janés, 2000), 138.

The settling on Marxism as the theory through which the young Ernesto found answers, according to his own reflections, was invariably accompanied by the ongoing presence of Karl Marx himself. This starting point explains why, at the height of his intellectual and revolutionary development, Che returned to Marx as a compass pointing the way to answers—some polemical, some definitive and others "simply" doubts about important matters related to socialism and the difficult transition to socialism, a transition that is fundamental in bringing about the transformation of human beings themselves. This became a personal quest when Che began to study humanist philosophy, first in a general way, until he finally found its true essence in Marxism.

This unpublished work on Marx and Engels, which Che called a "biographical synthesis," was written as a rough draft for a future book on political economy that Che felt was needed. It became a warning about how and where to begin an analysis of the emerging theoretical distortions concerning the process of transition to socialism and the terrible consequences of mistaken interpretations when they were put into practice.

That prevailing synthesis of theory and practice was an expression not only of the potential for revolutionary practice but also the necessity of organization and its reflection in theory, drawing on specific experiences in order to understand the subjective and objective factors that determine particular events.

Aware of the great challenge to write a book that would cover both the main propositions of political economy and past and future debates, Che warned: "Marx's statement in the first few pages of *Capital* about the inability of bourgeois science to criticize itself, using apologetics instead, can unfortunately be applied to Marxist economics today."*

Therefore, it was no accident that Che approached the polemic from the viewpoint of Marx and Engels, the latter not only being the cofounder of socialist theory but also the "first Marxist," who continued Marx's ideas after his death. The revolutionary thinking generated by the monumental size of their collective output and the importance of Marxism — not as an ideal model to be applied

---

* Ernesto Che Guevara, *Apuntes críticos a la Economía Política*, (Ocean Sur, 2006), 32.

mechanically but rather as a body of thought that is constantly developed, challenged and adapted — would be Che's path to understanding social reality and the struggle for the transformation of society, and to developing a theoretical framework that would be open to experience.

Apart from this project on political economy, begun in 1965 or 1966 in Tanzania and Prague after his internationalist mission in the Congo, Che embarked on another of equal importance on philosophy, similarly reflecting his political evolution and experiences.

The "testimony of my thwarted attempt," as he would call it, was interrupted by the pressing need to begin a process of change that had been his purest aspiration since his youth, when he decided to immerse himself in the realities of Latin America. At such decisive moments, he felt a need to resort to his intellectual training — as seen, for example, in the farewell letter he wrote to his parents, explaining that his Marxism was "deeply rooted and purified."

Even though he never stated this explicitly, he may well have found inspiration and parallels between some aspects of Marx's life and his own, such as the difficult decisions he had to make. For example, Che wrote:

> We should never forget that Marx was always a magnificent human being. He loved his wife and children very much but felt his life's work had to come ahead of them. It was painful for the exemplary husband and father that his two loves—his family and his dedication to the proletariat—were mutually exclusive. He tried to make them compatible, and fulfill his obligations to both, but his private correspondence reveals misgivings due to the poor and sometimes miserable circumstances to which his family was reduced.

This shows that Che neither wanted to nor could ignore the polemic about Marxism that was arising not only within the so-called socialist system but also among leftist intellectuals everywhere, a polemic that convulsed the world in the 1960s.

In a footnote, Che criticizes the French philosopher Louis Althusser, who argued that there was an "epistemological break" in Marx's work that represented a radical departure from his early writings. "Until that time [1845], Marx had been a political communist and a romantic philosopher. From then on, his political thought was combined with the curiosity of the scientific materialist that Marx became in his maturity."

Guevarian dialectics, in contrast, considered that Marxist philosophy contained precepts that were crucial to understanding the process of transformation that made human beings the real agents of change. This interrelationship between the subjective and the material world was fundamental to Marxism, and understanding the role each had to play, Che argued, was what distinguished it from other currents of thought.

Thus, when Che observed Marx's evolution, he emphasized 1849, the year in which Marx's exile and political persecution began. Che considered this to have been a time of reevaluation and study, preparation for Marx's future publication of many classic works on revolutionary theory.

In assessing the theoretical value of each of Marx's works, Che expressed his own views. Based on the experiences of the Cuban revolutionary process, he resisted making any generalizations or stating infallible truths about Marxism, but at the same time constantly sought to understand its universal application, especially from the viewpoint of a Third World revolution.

One of the main theses he formulated was developed from the experience of radical change in Cuba and addressed how this might apply to other underdeveloped countries after they achieved their definitive liberation from colonialism. Because of his tremendous grasp of theory and his practical experience, Che approached Marx from a unique perspective and was able to comprehend his greatness with no ambiguity, to think as Marx did and avoid mechanical repetition of his ideas.

Remarking on Marx's rigor, Che writes: "His extraordinarily meticulous spirit kept him from indulging in dreams or discussing any topic without basing his argument on unassailable logic."

Che learned from this exemplary man, and he followed him way beyond this introduction. Pursuing his travels, immersed in a hostile, grueling environment—in Bolivia, which he had first encountered with the eyes of a traveler in the 1950s but which he now saw as part of a long struggle—he again directed himself to study and meditation, reading a number of works that drew him back to the origins of Marxism. This leads us to think that

Che felt this was necessary both to understand the monumental nature of Marx's work—despite its imperfections—but also to understand the paths, risks and potential of the revolutionary forces that, even without formulas and instructions, would find the means to develop.

This book will help young people in today's turbulent, tragic world to really understand the man whose picture adorns so many T-shirts.

Many of Che's comments about Marx reveal the link between the biographer and his subject and might also refer to Che himself. For example, his observation:

> Such a humane man whose capacity for affection extended to all those suffering throughout the world, offering a message of committed struggle and indomitable optimism, has been distorted by history and turned into a stone idol.
>
> For his example to be even more luminous, we must rescue him and give him a human dimension... My outline simply serves as an introduction to his work and is dedicated to those who may not be acquainted with

Marxist economics and who may not know of the vicissitudes of its founders.

The footnotes in this book are from Che's original manuscript unless otherwise indicated. Endnotes have been added by the editors.

The editors

Karl Marx

Friedrich Engels

MARX & ENGELS

A biographical introduction

Ernesto Che Guevara

KARL MARX AND FRIEDRICH ENGELS were born close to each other in terms of both geography and time. Marx was born in Trier on May 5, 1818, and Engels in Bremen on November 28, 1820 — both cities in the German province of the Rhineland. But they lived in radically different environments and never knew each other in their early youth.

Karl Marx was the son of a Jewish lawyer who converted to Christianity, but his whole family was imbued with Hebrew religious traditions. Although not poor, he would have felt the stabs of racial prejudice. He studied jurisprudence in Bonn and later in Berlin, where his philosophical quest began. He obtained his doctorate of philosophy in Jena in 1841, presenting a study on Democritus and Epicurus for his thesis.

Friedrich Engels never graduated from college but went into his father's business instead. Nevertheless, after completing his military service, he took courses in philosophy in Berlin. He suffered economic privation all his life, and his main concern was to help support his friend Marx, who was always on the brink of poverty, and who single-mindedly dedicated himself to his scientific research and the organization of the working class.

While Marx's father had a liberal spirit and understood his son's concerns, Engels' family — especially his father — suffered greatly from Friedrich's adventures. Even as a child, Friedrich had rebelled against all dogma.

The first arms taken up by both Marx and Engels were of the literary kind — writing poetry that critics considered insignificant. But this youthful dabbling soon came to an end. As young men, the two were attracted by Hegel's philosophy and took part in the disquisitions of the young Hegelians.

Both were dazzled by Feuerbach, and independent of one another, they sought to advance his ideas by developing dialectical materialism in a unique, historic partnership between two extraordinary men that was also an infinitely loyal, perfect friendship.

There is little to say of their lives before they met. Only one other person is worth mentioning, because of the tremendous role she would play

"Both were dazzled by Feuerbach, and independent of one another, they sought to advance his ideas by developing dialectical materialism in a unique, historic partnership between two extraordinary men that was also an infinitely loyal, perfect friendship."

Karl Marx, 1839

Friedrich Engels, 1841

in Marx's life: JENNY VON WESTPHALEN.*
This woman was a member of the lesser German
nobility and constituted the other pillar of Marx's
life. In intellectual terms, she cannot be regarded
as much more than a blind admirer of her husband
and the person who copied his manuscripts. Nor
was she much of a housewife. Her greatness lay in
her acknowledgment of her husband's genius and
the need for him to develop it through his writing,
which meant her sacrificing the most intimate
dreams of a woman of her class.

She was accustomed to the party games, leisure
and economic comfort and tranquility of her social
position, and it can be said that she lost everything
when she tied herself indissolubly to Marx, an unwavering, intransigent revolutionary. Several of
their children died of causes directly or indirectly
attributable to the poverty in which they lived for
many years. Theirs was an exemplary marriage—
their youngest daughter [Eleanor] testified to the
strength of the bond between them in her descrip-
tion of how Marx, a sick old man, farewelled his
wife who was dying in agony from a malignant
tumor:

---

* Capitals in the original. [Editors' note]

**Engels and Marx with Marx's daughters
Jenny, Eleanor and Laura, 1860**

Mother lay in the big front room and the Moor [Marx] lay in the little room next to it. The two who had grown so used to each other, whose lives had completely intertwined, could no longer be in the same room together... The Moor got over his illness once again. I shall never forget the morning when he felt himself strong enough to get up and go into mother's room. It was as though they were young again together — she a loving girl and he an ardent youth starting out together through life, and not an old man shattered by ill-health and a dying old lady taking leave of each other forever.[1]

Three of their daughters — Jenny, Laura and Eleanor — lived to adulthood. Several other children died, but the one whose loss affected both parents the most was Edgar, who died when he was eight. He is frequently and longingly mentioned by both of them in their private letters.

Even though Marx's wife was not nearly as important an influence on his life as Engels, it is essential to comment on her, at least briefly. She was an extraordinary woman and his compañera throughout his adult life, and he outlived her by only a little over a year.

Marx's career as a political writer began with an article on censorship, which that same censorship prevented from being published. The article was written for *German Annals*, edited by [Arnold] Ruge, a friend from his youth, though the two would soon go their separate ways. Marx's important work began in the *Rheinische Zeitung*, of which he soon became editor. The young Engels also began to polish his arms dialectically in those two publications, writing under the name of Friedrich Oswald.

Rheinische Zeitung caused great irritation in reactionary circles, so the Prussian government decided to suppress it, establishing censorship as a first step. Marx relinquished the editorship when it became clear that the shareholders wanted to moderate his criticisms in an attempt to save the publication.

Marx and Engels met sometime in October 1842, when Marx had already broken with the young Hegelians but Engels had not. So their first meeting was rather cold and gave no hint of the identification that eventually united them over so many years.

In view of the impossibility of publishing *German*

Annals in Germany, Ruge and Marx decided to found *Deutsch-Französische Jahrbücher*, a magazine published in France. In the only issue to appear, Marx published "Introduction to *A Contribution to the Critique of Hegel's Philosophy of Right*," in which he did not break with his earlier convictions but began to seek an interpretation of social history. In that same magazine, Engels published "Outlines of a Critique of Political Economy," the first important attempt to tackle economics by one of the founders of Marxism.

Marx used his time in Paris to delve deeper into his study of history, reading bourgeois writers such as Thierry and Guizot, from whom he took a key theoretical concept: class struggle. Much later, in 1854, in a letter to Engels he wrote:

> A book that has interested me greatly is Thierry's *Histoire de la formation et du progress du Tiers État* [The History of the Formation of the Third Estate] of 1853. It is strange how this gentleman, the "father" of the "class struggle" in French historiography, inveighs in his preface against the "moderns" who, while also perceiving the antagonism between the bourgeoisie and proletariat, purport to

discover traces of such opposition as far back
as the history of the "Third Estate" prior to
1789.[2]

While acknowledging the intellectual and historic
merits of his predecessors, Marx pointed to the
critical defects in the ideology of the bourgeois
thinkers.

He stayed in France for a little over a year before
being forced to leave; he then took his family — now
enlarged by the birth of his oldest daughter — to
Brussels.

By the time Engels published his first article on
economics, Marx had already studied the subject,
approaching it from a philosophical point of view
determined by his Hegelian-Feuerbachian roots.
His notes from these studies are amazingly incisive,
but were not published until many years after Marx
and Engels were both dead. These notes became
known as the *Economic and Philosophical Manuscripts
of 1844*.

The first work on which they collaborated was
written nearly entirely by Marx: *The Holy Family*.
It is a conglomeration of philosophical criticism
(against the young Hegelians), literary criticism

and flashes of historical materialism. A large part of the book is dedicated to criticism of the critique that a young Hegelian made of *The Mysteries of Paris*, a long, poorly written novel by Eugène Sue that has long been forgotten. In a letter to Engels in 1867, Marx, who had reread their early book, wrote:

> I was pleasantly surprised to see that we don't need to be ashamed of this work, considering the effect the Feuerbach cult produces in one is now very comical.

The Condition of the Working Class in England offers another brilliant glimpse of Engels, who showed himself to be well on the road to fulfilling his creative potential even before he turned 25. In a letter to Engels in 1863, Marx said:

> Rereading your book has made me unhappily aware of the changes wrought by age. With what zest and passion, what boldness of vision and absence of all learned or scientific reservations, the subject is still attacked in these pages! And then, the very illusion that tomorrow or the day after, the result will actually spring to life as history lends the

whole thing a warmth, vitality and humor
with which the later "gray on gray" contrasts
damned unfavorably.[3]

As [Franz] Mehring noted, Engels caught the
main point of the matter more quickly than Marx
and outdid him, too, in the ease with which he
expressed himself, with straightforward, smooth
flowing prose. But his writings give the impression
that he didn't like to elaborate too much on a subject, preferring instead to adopt a "journalistic" approach and to treat the topic, while not superficially,
in far less depth than Marx. His main works are
polemical fragments of thought, such as *Anti-
Dühring* (a philosopher saved from oblivion by this
title) and *Origin of the Family, Private Property and
the State* — which, though little more than a series of
footnotes, have been very important in the history
of Marxist thought.

Engels himself recognized this; whether in
absolute sincerity or with a touch of ironic self-
deprecation, in 1851 he wrote to Marx:

Anyhow, your new thing about land rent is
absolutely right. The increasing infertility of
the land concomitant with an ever-increasing

population in Ricardo has always seemed to me implausible, nor have I ever been able to discover any evidence in support of his ever-rising price of corn, but with my notorious sloth in matters of theory, I have silenced the inward grumbling of my better self and never gone to the root of the matter.[4]

Marx got there a little later, but his mighty humanity was engaged in traversing the path indefatigably—up and down, down and up, following every offshoot—without losing sight of the main road and never becoming disheartened, an effort eventually crowned with the achievement of *Capital*. His entire life and work were preparation for that masterly production.

In Brussels, the two partners wrote a new manuscript, *The German Ideology*, another of their unborn children that came to light only after the deaths of its progenitors. This replicates the tumultuous phraseology of *The Holy Family*, the erudite irony that makes it difficult for today's humble readers to understand the succession of broadsides against those who proved to be dwarfs forgotten by history. This book presented a view of

"Marx got there a little later, but his mighty humanity was engaged in traversing the path indefatigably—up and down, down and up, following every offshoot—without losing sight of the main road and never becoming disheartened, an effort eventually crowned with the achievement of *Capital*."

society as a great synthesis in continuous change, with violent upheavals and with characteristics particular to each period. It reveals a concrete preoccupation with social problems that brought Marx and Engels close to the communists of the period and also to [Pierre-Joseph] Proudhon— whom they criticized sharply. Their criticism of the "modern socialists," members of a type of philosophical sect who pretended to be above political squabbles on a plane of pure thought, is both accurate and pitiless.*

The concord between such opposed characters as Proudhon and Marx, who held such contradictory visions of society, could not last.

---

* Marx considered *The German Ideology* to be important, be- cause it meant "settling accounts with our former political conscience." When difficulties arose for its publication, they "abandoned the manuscript to the gnawing criticism of the mice all the more willingly since we had achieved our main purpose—self-clarification." (Marx, Preface to *A Contribution to the Critique of Political Economy*)

For his part, [Louis] Althusser considered it marked an "epistemological break" in Marx's work that represented a radical departure from his early writings. Until that time [1845], Marx had been a political communist and a romantic philosopher. From then on, his political thought was com- bined with the curiosity of the scientific materialist that Marx became in his maturity.

Proudhon wrote *The Philosophy of Poverty*, and Marx responded with *The Poverty of Philosophy*. This polemical work, which made the rivals enemies for life, was important because it was the first presentation of a complete outline of historical materialism. There was still a long way to go to complete his work, but it set forth the essential points. So passed the year 1847.

In a letter to P.V. Annenkov dated December 28, 1846, Marx summarized his criticism of Proudhon, from which these paragraphs are extracted:

> To be frank, I must admit that I find the book on the whole poor, if not very poor. You yourself make fun in your letter of the "little bit of German philosophy" paraded by Mr. Proudhon in this amorphous and overweening work, but you assume that the economic argument has remained untainted by the philosophic poison. Therefore I am by no means inclined to ascribe the faults of the economic argument to Mr. Proudhon's philosophy. Mr. Proudhon does not provide a false critique of political economy because his philosophy is absurd—he produces an absurd philosophy because he has not

understood present social conditions in their *engrènement* [intermeshing], to use a word which Mr. Proudhon borrows from Fourier, like so much else...

What is society, irrespective of its form? The product of man's interaction upon man. Is man free to choose this or that form of society? By no means. If you assume a given state of development of man's productive faculties, you will have a corresponding form of commerce and consumption. If you assume given stages of development in production, commerce and consumption, you will have a corresponding form of social constitution, a corresponding organization, whether of the family, of the estates or of the classes—in a word, a corresponding civil society. If you assume this or that civil society, you will have this or that political system, which is but the official expression of civil society. This is something Mr. Proudhon will never understand, for he imagines he's doing something great when he appeals from the state to civil society, i.e. to official society from the official epitome of society.

Needless to say, man is not free to choose

his productive forces — upon which his whole history is based — for every productive force is an acquired force, the product of previous activity...

In England, all the earlier economic forms, the social relations corresponding to them and the political system, which was the official expression of the old civil society, were destroyed. Thus, the economic forms in which man produces, consumes and exchanges are *transitory and historical*. With the acquisition of new productive faculties, man changes his mode of production and with the mode of production he changes all the economic relations which were but necessary relations of that particular mode of production...

Mr. Proudhon understands perfectly well that men manufacture worsted, linens and silks; and whatever credit is due for understanding such a trifle! What Mr. Proudhon does not understand is that, according to their faculties, men also produce the *social relations* in which they produce worsted and linens. Still less does Mr. Proudhon understand that those who produce social relations in conformity with their material productivity also produce the *ideas, categories*, i.e. the ideal abstract expressions of those same social relations. Indeed, the categories are no more eternal than the relations they express. They are historical and transitory products. To Mr. Proudhon, on the contrary, the prime cause consists in abstractions and categories. According to him, it is these and not men that make history. *The abstraction, the category regarded as such*, i.e. as distinct from man and his material activity, is, of course, immortal, immutable, impassive. It is nothing but an entity of pure reason, which is only another way of saying that an abstraction, regarded as such, is abstract. An admirable tautology![5]

In Brussels, the already inseparable friends, together with other young communists, among whom [Wilhelm] Wolff was the most outstanding, dedicated themselves to creating a center for organizing the communist associations that were scattered throughout Europe. A year later [in 1848], as the fruit of their coordinating activity, they published a document of key importance: *The Communist Manifesto*.

This work was still immature in its concepts

and timid in its stated aspirations. It had a critical
appendix of socialist literature, to which it added
nothing and which, in our opinion, took away
much of the vitality of the proclamation. But, even
today, when so many parties and left groups hide
their real aspirations (or what should be their real
aspirations) behind an insipid philosophy filled
with "understanding" toward the "more reason-
able" elements of the exploiting classes, any revolutionary pledging themselves to *The Communist
Manifesto* need not fear they will be considered half-
hearted. In 1848, it was a truly audacious document
and probably would have been brutally suppressed
if it had not been for the fact that little attention was
paid to the recently founded Communist League,
the organization that assigned Marx to write the
Manifesto — which he did in close collaboration with
Engels.

During that period, Marx and Engels continued
to deepen their knowledge of political economy.

Supported by the wave of revolutionary senti-
ment that swept Europe in 1848, they also became
totally involved in German politics, founding the
Neue Rheinische Zeitung in Cologne. They worked
tirelessly for nearly a year, promoting the German

people's revolutionary spirit through that magazine and other publications such as that of the Communist Party of Germany that followed the line of *The Communist Manifesto*.

The reactionaries gained confidence as they rained blows on the still immature proletariat, and finally they felt strong enough to attack their most potent ideological foe: the *Neue Rheinische Zeitung*. On May 12, 1849, an order was issued expelling Marx and several other contributors to the publication* from Germany. On May 19, its last issue was published—in red ink, with some verses by [Ferdinand] Freiligrath that became quite famous. The revolutionary poet maintained a great friendship with Marx until his enthusiasm gave way to nostalgia for his native land (he lived in exile in London for many years) and his relations with him cooled over the Vogt case, to which I will refer later on.

Marx and Engels' friendship with Ferdinand Lassalle also dated from that period. Though it

---

* The editorial staff of the *Neue Rheinische Zeitung* consisted of Karl Marx as editor in chief, [Heinrich] Bürgers, [Ernst] Dronke, [Friedrich] Engels, [Georg] Weerth, [Ferdinand] Wolff and [Wilhelm] Wolff.

Karl Marx

ebbed and flowed due to Lassalle's defects, this friendship would last until his sudden death, after which Marx and Engels had to struggle resolutely against Lassalle's followers, whose tactics of struggle eventually led to revisionism. Marx always had a poor opinion of Lassalle's grasp of economics and also—though not to the same extent—of his philosophical depth. In a letter to Engels in 1858, commenting on *Heracles the Obscure*, which Lassalle had just published, Marx wrote:

> It is plain to me… that, in his second grand opus, the fellow intends to expound political economy in the manner of Hegel. He will discover to his cost that it is one thing for a critique to take a science to the point at which it admits of a dialectical presentation, and quite another to apply an abstract, ready-made system of logic to vague presentiments of just such a system.[6]

The two friends, however, valued him for his having united the German proletariat. When Lassalle was killed in a duel over a woman in September 1864, Engels wrote Marx:

You can imagine how surprised I was by the news. Whatever Lassalle may have been in other respects as a person, writer, scholar — he was, as a politician, undoubtedly one of the most significant men in Germany. For us he was a very uncertain friend now and would, in future, most certainly have been our enemy; but nevertheless, it's very galling to see how Germany destroys all those in the extreme party who are in any way worth their salt. What jubilation there will be among the manufacturers and among the Progress swine, for L. was indeed the only man actually inside Germany of whom they were afraid.[7]

For his part, Marx made no criticism of their dead friend at this time, although he severely castigated him several years later when he learned of some of his maneuvers with Bismarck.

Responding — somewhat belatedly — to the [1848] revolutionary wave, the German masses rose up in arms, especially in Baden and the Palatinate, and Engels rushed there to enlist as a soldier. The terror that his name, which was becoming quite well known publicly, inspired in the bourgeoisie — which was always lying in wait to profit from the struggle without risking anything—prevented him from playing an outstanding leadership role. Nevertheless, as [Prussian military officer August] Willich's aide in his voluntary exile, he took part in four battles that were waged to protect the defeated Baden army's withdrawal to Switzerland. His military experience lasted for a month, from June 13 to July 12, 1849, the date on which he crossed the border with his detachment, the last in the withdrawal. He would retain his passion for a military career all his life and took responsibility for writing on military topics whenever Marx had to refer to them in his articles.

Soon afterwards, while living in France, Marx received an order exiling him to an isolated, unhealthy part of Brittany. He moved instead to London, which would be his permanent place of residence for the rest of his life.

Undaunted, Marx and Engels founded the *Neue Rheinische Zeitung* in the English capital. Marx was editor of the magazine, of which six issues were published. In it, he brought his characteristic depth and ever greater mastery of his subject to bear on the political questions of the day and on the activities of the Communist League, which was unable

Cover of the text used by Che Guevara

to survive the decline of the 1848 revolutionary upsurge. Marx and Engels also used its pages to confront Engels' old commanding officer, Willich, who had developed political differences with the future leaders of the world proletariat.

After the magazine folded, Engels settled in Manchester [England] as the representative of the textile factory of which his father was co-owner, while Marx remained in London, near the British Museum, whose archives he consulted in his scientific work.

A friend of theirs, [Joseph] Weydemeyer, had to emigrate to the United States to escape persecution and founded a short-lived magazine there which was important for the publication of *The Eighteenth Brumaire of Louis Bonaparte* in its pages. This political analysis is still profound and convincing today, but Marx's conclusions were too radical for that era, so it was not a successful publication. In contrast, the analyses of "little Napoleon" (as Victor Hugo called him) by Hugo and Proudhon, who had written on this same subject previously, were well received among the reading public.

Those were times of summing up and study. Marx published *The Class Struggles in France, 1848-50* and *The Eighteenth Brumaire of Louis Bonaparte*. For his part, Engels wrote *The Peasant War in Germany* and *Revolution and Counterrevolution in Germany*. Marx and Engels maintained that it was necessary to wait for better revolutionary conditions, and this clashed with the blind fervor of Willich, who was in favor of action at all costs. Marx and Engels finally parted company with the group of émigrés and their sterile quarrels that distracted them from the scientific task they had set themselves. At Marx's suggestion, the Communist League declared itself dissolved in November 1852.

That period in London was one of the hardest in Marx's life. His friend Engels was unable to help him as much as he wanted to, because he had to maintain his own household with Mary Burns, an Irish girl who was Engels' compañera until his death.

The articles Marx wrote for the *New York Tribune* — which didn't always publish them (and, when it didn't, didn't pay for them, either) — were his only source of income. The Marx family were unable to live on the money received for those articles and, as already mentioned, neither Marx nor his wife was adept at the prosaic daily art of

Karl Marx

Karl Marx and Eleanor, 1869

pinching pennies and making each one stretch as far as possible.

Their son Edgar died during that period, in 1855, leaving many distressing memories for the rest of their marriage. We should never forget that Marx was always a magnificent human being. He loved his wife and children very much but felt his life's work had to come ahead of them. It was painful for the exemplary husband and father that his two loves — his family and his dedication to the proletariat — were mutually exclusive. He tried to make them compatible, and fulfill his obligations to both, but his private correspondence reveals misgivings due to the poor and sometimes miserable circumstances to which his family was reduced.

In a letter to [Ludwig] Kugelmann in 1862, he wrote:

> In 1861, I lost my chief source of income, the *New York Tribune*, as a result of the American Civil War. My contributions to that paper have remained in abeyance up to the present. Thus, I have been, and still am, forced to undertake a large amount of hackwork to prevent myself and my family from actually

being relegated to the streets. I had even decided to become a "practical man" and had intended to enter a railway office at the beginning of next year. Luckily—or perhaps I should say unluckily?—I did not get the post because of my bad handwriting. So you will see that I had little time left and few quiet moments for theoretical work.[8]

In 1867, he wrote to Meyer—a letter which is exceptional for its emotional tone—turning furiously on everything:

Well, why didn't I answer you? Because I was constantly hovering at the edge of the grave. Hence I had to make use of *every* moment when I was able to work to complete my book to which I have sacrificed my health, happiness and family. I trust that I need not add anything to this explanation. I laugh at the so-called "practical" men with their wisdom. If one chose to be an ox, one could of course turn one's back on the sufferings of mankind and look after one's own skin. But I should really have regarded myself as *impractical* if I had pegged out without completely finishing my book, at least in manuscript.[9]

In 1859, Marx finished a part of his economic work, publishing *A Contribution to the Critique of Political Economy*, but it was only a variation of, an antecedent to, *Capital*. It included the study of commodities and money, a part of Volume I of his masterpiece. However, the prose is much heavier in this first work, which explains the success of the criticism it received and why even Lassalle failed to read its real content, which would not have been the case if he had seen the treatment given to the subject in the finished work. At first, the work was to be published in pamphlets, in six sections. Time and Marx's delving deeper into his studies changed that plan. In a letter written to Engels in 1858, he explained:

> The following is a short outline of the first part. The whole thing is divided into six books: 1. On Capital (contains a few introductory chapters). 2. Landed Property. 3. Wage Labor. 4. State. 5. International Trade. 6. World Market.
>
> *Capital* falls into four sections: a/ Capital in general. (This is the substance of the first installment.) b/ *Competition*, or the interaction of many capitals. c/ *Credit*, where capital, as

against individual capitals, is shown to be a universal element. d/ *Share capital* as the most perfected form (turning into communism) together with all its contradictions.[10]

Marx was eager to finish his work on economics, for, as he himself said, he was growing tired of that science, which had advanced so little since Smith and Ricardo. However, one of his basic discoveries was proclaimed (though not proved, since the publication of his pamphlets was halted): the mechanism of value, including the concept of labor power, a subtlety which would enable him to explain the complicated mechanism of the capitalist relations of production and their result: surplus value.

Although not elaborated, this is presented in the following paragraph:

If the exchange value of a commodity is equal to the amount of labor time it contains, the exchange value of one day's labor is equal to what that labor produces. That is to say, the wage paid for labor has to be equal to the product of that labor. But, in fact, the contrary is true. Ergo. This poses the question: How can

> the exchange value of a commodity created
> by labor be greater than the cost of that labor,
> unless the exchange value of labor is less than
> the exchange value it creates. We will resolve
> this matter by studying the nature of capital
> itself.

But this part didn't see the light of day until eight years later, in the final version of *Capital*.

Shortly after the partial publication of his work, due to a series of intrigues, Marx was forced to write a polemical pamphlet, *Herr Vogt*. In it, he showed just who that man—who had defamed him—was: an agent of Napoleon. He was one of the many characters who obtained a place in history thanks to their having been criticized by Marx and Engels, which made people interested to find out who they were. Vogt added nothing to the science of economics or to Marx's reputation.

Marx spent the next few years working on his basic tasks: *Capital* and the First International [the International Working Men's Association]. It was founded in London in 1864, and Marx wrote the inaugural address and its statutes.

The First International was short-lived, considering its character, but was of great importance in the organization of the working class. Errors by the German followers of Lassalle and continual disagreements with the supporters of Proudhon and Bakunin finally turned it into a hotbed of intrigue. Even so, its demise was due to lack of support from organized European workers—some of whom, especially the English working class, began to receive the crumbs which imperialism distributed to the exploited class of its own country when it found other places in which to engage in unbridled plundering.

In the revolutionary ebb that followed the [1871] Paris Commune, the first international workers' association collapsed—but not before alarming the reactionaries, who began to take quick containment measures.*

---

* The following paragraph from a letter that Engels wrote to [Friedrich Adolf] Sorge in 1874 brings out the exact role the International played in the Paris events: "Actually in 1864 the theoretical character of the movement was still very unclear everywhere in Europe, that is, among the masses. German communism did not yet exist as a workers party, Proudhonism was too weak to be able to trot out its particular hobby horses, Bakunin's new balderdash had not so much come into being in his own head, and even the leaders of the English trade unions thought the program laid down in the preamble to the rules gave them a basis for

The Franco-German conflict and the subsequent Paris Commune clearly showed the nature of bourgeois wars. The victorious Germans and defeated French exploiters were not loath to join forces to ruthlessly wipe out the first serious attempt of the proletariat to "storm the heavens," as Marx put it.

The Franco-Prussian war began on July 19, 1870. On July 23, the General Council of the International published a special call—written by Marx— warning European workers about the nature and purpose of the war.

After Sedan, Marx didn't think that the proletariat would really take power, but, when it did, he gave it his determined support. The International had nothing to do with that rather spontaneous action of the masses, who were in open rebellion or, in any case, under the influence of the Blanquists, but it assumed the defense of the

---

entering the movement. The first great success was bound to explode this naïve conjunction of all factions. This success was the [Paris] Commune, which was without any doubt the child of the International intellectually, although the International did not lift a finger to produce it, and for which the International to a certain extent was quite properly held responsible."

vanquished and took up their cause—naturally, influenced by Marx and Engels. This polarized the hatred of the bourgeoisie and the distrust of all the members of the working class who, in one way or another, had an interest in perpetuating the status quo. The English workers broke with the International, and it was dissolved soon afterward. The only testament it left was an unwavering faith in the future of socialist society.

For their part, Marx and Engels learned from the failure, and Marx made a profound analysis of the events in *The Civil War in France*, published under the auspices of the International. One of the most important consequences of the Commune was the light it shed on the need to destroy the old governmental apparatus in order to consolidate the people's power.

The polemic on this point continues even now. In a letter to his friend [Ludwig] Kugelmann, Marx said that it might not be necessary to destroy all of the previous governmental apparatus in England. Just before the October [Russian] revolution, Lenin noted the "historically extraordinary" possibility of seizing power by peaceful means. These two phrases, taken out of context or tendentiously interpreted, have served for the defense of the "aggress-ive pacifism" of many leaders of communist parties and even socialist nations.

In any case, Marx's opinion on the mistakes and successes of the Commune was categorical, as evident in another letter to Kugelmann, dated April 12, 1871, and some other letters:

> If you look at the last chapter of my *Eighteenth Brumaire*, you will find that I declare that the next attempt of the French revolution will be no longer, as before, to transfer the bureau-cratic-military machine from one hand to another, but to *smash* it, and this is the pre-liminary condition for every real people's revolution on the Continent. And this is what our heroic party comrades in Paris are attempting. What elasticity, what historical initiative, what a capacity for sacrifice in these Parisians! After six months of hunger and ruin, caused by internal treachery even more than by the external enemy, they rise, beneath Prussian bayonets, as if there had never been a war between France and Germany and the enemy were not still at the gates of Paris! History has no like example of like greatness!

If they are defeated, only their "good nature" will be to blame. They should have marched at once on Versailles after first Vinoy and then the reactionary section of the Paris National Guard had themselves retreated. They missed their opportunity because of conscientious scruples. They did not want *to start a civil war*, as if that mischievous abortion Thiers had not already started the civil war with his attempt to disarm Paris! Second mistake: The Central Committee surrendered its power too soon, to make way for the Commune. Again from a too "honorable" scrupulosity! However that may be, the present rising in Paris — even if it be crushed by the wolves, swine and vile curs of the old society — is the most glorious deed of our party since the June insurrection in Paris.[11]

In 1867, Marx saw part of his work crowned with the publication of the completed first volume of *Capital*. The other volumes weren't published until after his death and didn't complete his economic thought, since some entire parts — such as the section on international trade, which would have allowed him at least to examine the nascent

**Cover of the edition of *Capital*
consulted by Che Guevara**

Carlos Marx
El Capital (1ª Edición cubana)
Tomo I

Prólogo a la primera edición

"En el análisis de las formas económicas de nada sirven el microscopio ni los reactivos químicos. El único medio de que disponemos, en este terreno, es la capacidad de abstracción. La forma de mercancía que adopta el producto del trabajo o la forma de valor que reviste la mercancía es la célula económica de la sociedad soviética   [XXI - XXII]"

"Las naciones pueden y deben escarmentar en cabeza ajena. Aunque una sociedad haya encontrado el rastro de la ley natural con arreglo a la cual se mueve — y la finalidad última de esta obra es, en efecto, descubrir la ley económica que preside el movimiento de la sociedad moderna —, jamás podrá saltar ni descartar por decreto las fases naturales de su desarrollo. Podrá únicamente acortar y mitigar los dolores del parto." [XXIII]

Che's notes on *Capital*

imperialist phenomenon — were missing.

In a letter to Kugelmann in 1866 [October 13], he had set forth the plan of the work, which was very similar to the final result that has come down to us in incomplete form:

> The complete work is divided as follows:
>
> Book One: The Process of Production of Capital
>
> Book Two: The Process of Circulation of Capital
>
> Book Three: The Structure of the Process as a Whole
>
> Book Four: A Contribution to the History of Economic Theory

The rest of this book is a summary of *Capital* and its critical analysis, so we won't go into this now, other than to quote a letter that Marx wrote to Engels in 1867, in which he outlined the most important aspects, as he saw them:

> The best points in my book are: 1. the *two-fold character of labor*, according to whether it is expressed in the use of value or exchange

value. (*All* understanding of the facts depends upon this.) It is emphasized immediately, in the *first* chapter; 2. the treatment of *surplus value independently of its particular* forms as profit, interest, rent, etc. This will be seen especially in the second volume. The treatment of the particular forms by classical economy, which always mixes them up with the general form, is a regular hash.[12]

This was his last period of peak creativity, when he wrote a large part of the other two volumes and of the *Theories of Surplus Value*.

In his final years, he left one other important work, a ray of light about the future that he called *Critique of the Gotha Program*, the only more or less organic prediction that he made about the communist future. His extraordinarily meticulous spirit kept him from indulging in dreams or discussing any topic without basing his argument on unassailable logic. It was his indignation over the program of the German Social Democrats (who had fallen under the influence of Lassalle's followers) that made him decide to write on this subject, and then only in the form of an analysis of that program.

Ever weaker, though free of economic worries, thanks to his comrade Engels, Marx spent his last few years suffering from the loss of his two Jennys—mother and daughter—who died in December 1881 and early 1883, respectively. Unable to work and lacking the secret source of his energy, which he had lost with their deaths, there was nothing left for him to do but withdraw from the world on March 14, 1883.

Such a humane man whose capacity for affection extended to all those suffering throughout the world, offering a message of committed struggle and indomitable optimism, has been distorted by history and turned into a stone idol.

For his example to be even more luminous, we must rescue him and give him a human dimension. Marxism is still waiting for the biography that will complete Mehring's magnificent work[13] with greater perspective and correct the few mistakes in interpretation from which it suffers. My outline is simply an introduction to his work, dedicated to those who may not be acquainted with Marxist economics and who may not know of the vicissitudes of its founders.

"Such a humane man whose capacity for affection extended to all those suffering throughout the world, offering a message of committed struggle and indomitable optimism, has been distorted by history and turned into a stone idol."

In any case, Engels' address at Marx's tomb summed up his life:

> On the afternoon of the 14th of March at a quarter to three the greatest living thinker ceased to think. Left alone for less than two minutes, when we entered we found him sleeping peacefully in his chair — but forever.
>
> It is impossible to measure the loss which the fighting European and American proletariat and historical science has lost with the death of this man. Soon enough we shall feel the breach which has been broken by the death of this tremendous spirit.
>
> As Darwin discovered the law of evolution in organic nature, so Marx discovered the law of evolution in human history: the simple fact, previously hidden under ideological growths, that human beings must first of all eat, drink, shelter and clothe themselves before they can turn their attention to politics, science, art and religion; that therefore the production of the immediate material means of life and consequently the given stage of economic development of a people or of a period forms the basis on which the state institutions, the legal

principles, the art and even the religious ideas of the people in question have developed and out of which they must be explained, instead of exactly the contrary, as was previously attempted.

But not only this, Marx discovered the special law of development of the present-day capitalist mode of production and of the bourgeois system of society which it has produced. With the discovery of surplus value light was suddenly shed on the darkness in which all other economists, both bourgeois and socialist, had been groping.

Two such discoveries would have been enough for any life. Fortunate indeed is he to whom it is given to make even one, but on every single field which Marx investigated (and there were many and on none of them were his investigations superficial) he made independent discoveries, even on the field of mathematics.

That was the man of science, but that was by no means the whole man. For Marx, science was a creative, historic and revolutionary force. Great as was his pleasure at a new discovery on this or that field of theoretical science, a discovery perhaps whose practical consequences were not yet visible, it was still greater at a new discovery which immediately affected industrial development, historical development as a whole, in a revolutionary fashion. For instance, he closely followed the development of the discoveries on the field of electrical science and towards the end the work of Marcel Deprez.

For Marx was above all a revolutionary, and his great aim in life was to cooperate in this or that fashion in the overthrow of capitalist society and the state institutions which it has created, to cooperate in the emancipation of the modern proletariat, to whom he was the first to give a consciousness of its class position and its class needs, a knowledge of the conditions necessary for its emancipation. In this struggle he was in his element, and he fought with a passion and tenacity and with a success granted to few. The first *Rheinische Zeitung* in 1842, the *Vorwärts* in Paris in 1844, the *Deutsche Brüsseler Zeitung* in 1847, the *Neue Rheinische Zeitung* from 1848 to 1849, the *New York Tribune* from 1852 to 1861 — and then a wealth of polemical writings, the organizational work in Paris, Brussels and London, and finally the great International Working Men's Association to crown it all. In truth, that alone would have been a life's work to be proud of if its author had done nothing else.

And therefore Marx was the best-hated and most slandered man of his age. Governments, both absolutist and republican, expelled him from their territories, whilst the bourgeois, both conservative and extreme-democratic, vied with each other in a campaign of vilification against him. He brushed it all to one side like cobwebs, ignored them and answered only when compelled to do so. And he died honored, loved and mourned by millions of revolutionary workers from the Siberian mines over Europe and America to the coasts of California, and I make bold to say that although he had many opponents, he had hardly a personal enemy.

His name will live through the centuries and so will his work.[14]

After Marx's death, Engels had to defend Marxist theory in all its aspects — a defense that he continued as long as he lived.

"Marx was the best-hated and most slandered man of his age. [But] he died honored, loved and mourned by millions of revolutionary workers from the Siberian mines over Europe and America to the coasts of California... His name will live through the centuries and so will his work."
—Engels on Marx

Years earlier, when a series of articles expressing a Proudhonist point of view on housing was published in the Social Democratic press in Germany, Engels wrote *The Housing Question*, making a Marxist approach to the topic (1872–73).

In 1877, he began to publish a series of articles refuting [Eugen] Dühring, a socialist philosopher who was held in great esteem by members of the party. Later, the articles were made into a book, the famous *Anti-Dühring*. That book, whose chapter on political economy was written by Marx, contained a broad, quite complete presentation of Marxist ideas on the world as a whole and, together with *Dialectics of Nature* – which, unfortunately, he didn't manage to finish – was a very useful complement to *Capital*.

Engels began this last book in the 1870s. He interrupted it to write *Anti-Dühring* and then never completed it. It remained as a legacy for German Social Democracy, which either didn't consider it useful or feared it (probably the latter). The Soviet Union rescued it for posterity, and it was printed there for the first time in 1925.

Engels had the enormous task of completing *Capital*, which was his greatest concern. Volume

II, whose prologue stated that Volume III would be appearing soon, was published relatively quickly, in 1885, just two years after Marx's death. However, it took Engels 10 years to compile the mass of manuscripts Marx had left, and he wasn't able to publish them until a few months before his own death.

While still a loyal Marxist, the Social Democrat Karl Kautsky undertook the task of publishing the *Critical History of the Theory of Surplus Value*. This work was a collection of Marx's criticisms of earlier and contemporary writings. It added nothing new to the theory but showed the development of some obscure points, such as crises—a topic that I don't believe Marx and his followers studied with the required depth.

In 1884, Engels published *Origin of the Family, Private Property and the State*, basing himself on Marx's critical analyses of the US researcher Morgan's *Primitive Society* and on his own studies. It was a brilliant exposition of the development of society which cleared up the historical origins of the social categories, showing that they had specific beginnings—which presupposed their end in certain circumstances. The somewhat earlier research done by Morgan and by Darwin confirmed the philosophical concepts of dialectical materialism.

In 1886, Engels wrote *Ludwig Feuerbach and the End of German Classical Philosophy*, which was also the result of polemical articles stemming from a book that Starkey wrote on Feuerbach.

Above all, the amount of correspondence that Engels maintained in a dozen languages—he was a veritable polyglot—was amazing. In this respect, his work made a substantial contribution to Marxism in numerous instances. Moreover, his letters always showed him to be a thoroughly consistent revolutionary who tried to ensure that the proletarian parties—which were sometimes swayed by revisionist ideas that had their greatest exponents in [Eduard] Bernstein and German Social Democracy, to which he belonged—would hold fast to correct concepts. It was sad that the German Social Democrats fell victim to those ideas, because their party was considered the most advanced one, with the greatest possibilities for seizing power.

Engels never evinced any enthusiasm over the projected creation of the Second International [in 1881], because he did not consider the time was

"It is interesting to note that this proponent of scientific socialism [Engels], a materialist to the marrow of his bones, made the romantic gesture of leaving instructions in his will that his ashes be thrown into the North Sea at one of his favorite places on the coast."

ripe. Nevertheless, faced with the possibility that an opportunist organization was being created behind the backs of the proletariat, he participated in the preliminary work for the Paris congress at which the Second International was formally constituted. One of the historically significant resolutions of that association was the declaration of May 1 as the day of international celebration of the proletariat in homage to the martyrs of Chicago [1886].

His eyes were always alert and his pen ready to join the fray to defend the purity of theory and, we must stress, a revolutionary stand. Thus, at the end of his life, he harshly criticized the French socialists in an article, "The Peasant Question in France and Germany," because they were adapting their program to suit the aspirations of small farmers.

Engels died on August 5, 1895, at the age of 75, the victim of cancer that had made the last few months of his life an agony.

It is interesting to note that this proponent of scientific socialism, a materialist to the marrow of his bones, made the romantic gesture of leaving instructions in his will that his ashes be thrown into the North Sea at one of his favorite places on the coast.

With his death, the circle was closed. Only when Lenin appeared did another open, with an even greater practical effect—the liberation of the proletariat.

<u>Indice</u>

~~Obras~~

Marx - Engels - Obras ~~políticas~~ escogidas

Tomo I 1

   Manifiesto del partido comunista (Marx-Engels) ... 1

   Trabajo asalariado y Capital (Marx) ... 7

   Las luchas de clase en Francia de 1848 a 1850, ... 9
   (Marx, prólogo de Engels)

   El 18 brumario de Luis Bonaparte (Marx) ... 12

   Futuro resultado de la dominación británica
   en la India (Marx) ... 12

   Prólogo de la contribución a la crítica de
   la economía política (Marx) ... 14

Tomo II ... 15

   Salario, precio y ganancia (Marx) ... 15

   Prefacio del Capital (Marx) ... 20

   El Capital de Marx (Engels) ... 20

   La guerra civil en Francia (Marx) ... 21

   Acerca de las relaciones sociales en Rusia ... 23
   (Engels)

   Introducción a la dialéctica de la natura-
   leza (Engels) ... 26

   Prólogo al folleto, del socialismo utópico

Che's suggested reading list

Carlos Marx – Federico Engels
Obras escojidas en tres tomos
(Editora política, Habana, 1963)
TOMO I

" La historia de todas las sociedades que han existido
hasta nuestros días es la historia de la lucha de cla-
ses"
(Marx-Engels, Manifiesto del partido comunista, 1848 [pg. 21])

[la burguesía] "Ha hecho " de la dignidad personal un
simple valor de cambio "
(Marx - Engels, Ibid [pg. 24]

"La burguesía no puede existir sino a condición
de revolucionar incesantemente los instrumentos de producción
y, por consiguiente, las relaciones de producción, y con
ello todas las relaciones sociales"
(Marx - Engels, Ibid [pg. 25])

"El lumpenproletariado, ese producto pasivo de la putre-
facción de las capas más bajas de la ~~sociedad~~ vieja
sociedad, puede a veces ser arrastrado al movimiento

Che's notes on Marx & Engels
Selected Works

Notes

1. Quoted by Franz Mehring, *Karl Marx*, (Ann Arbor: Ann Arbor Paperbacks, 1962), 528

2. Marx to Engels, July 27, 1854, in *Karl Marx Frederick Engels Collected Works, Vol. 39, 1852–1855*, (London: Lawrence & Wishart), 473

3. Marx to Engels, April 18, 1863, in *Karl Marx Frederick Engels Collected Works, Vol. 41, 1860–1864*, 469

4. Engels to Marx, January 29, 1851, in *Karl Marx Frederick Engels Collected Works, Vol. 38 1844–1851*, 270–71

5. Marx to Pavel Vasilyevich Annenkov, December 28, 1846, in *Karl Marx Frederick Engels Collected Works, Vol. 38, 1844–1851*, 95–102

6. Marx to Engels, February 1, 1858, in *Karl Marx Frederick Engels Collected Works, Vol. 40, 1856–1859*, 261

7. Engels to Marx, September 4, 1864, in *Karl Marx Frederick Engels Collected Works, Vol. 41, 1860–1864,* 558

8. Marx to Ludwig Kugelmann, December 28, 1862, in *Karl Marx Frederick Engels Collected Works, Vol. 41, 1860–1864,* 435–36

9. Marx to Siegfried Meyer, April 30, 1867, in *Marx Engels, Selected Correspondence* (Moscow: Progress Publishers, 1975), 173

10. Marx to Engels, April 2, 1858, in *Karl Marx Frederick Engels Collected Works, Vol. 40, 1856–1859,* 298

11. Marx to Ludwig Kugelmann, April 12, 1871, in *Marx Engels, Selected Correspondence, op. cit.,* 284

12. Marx to Engels, August 24, 1867, in *Marx Engels, Selected Correspondence, op. cit.,* 180

13. Franz Mehring, *Karl Marx, op. cit.*

14. Quoted by Franz Mehring, *Karl Marx, op. cit.,* 531–32

Che's reading list on Marx and Engels

Karl Marx

- Introduction to *A Contribution to the Critique of Hegel's Philosophy of Right* (1844)
- *Economic and Philosophical Manuscripts* (1844, published in 1932)
- *The Holy Family* or *Critique of Critical Criticism. Against Bruno Bauer and Company* (1845) written with Engels
- *The German Ideology* (1845) written with Engels
- *The Poverty of Philosophy* (1847)
- *Wage Labor and Capital* (1847)
- *Manifesto of the Communist Party* (1848) written with Engels

- *The Class Struggles in France 1848–50* (1850, published in 1895)
- *The Eighteenth Brumaire of Louis Bonaparte* (1852)
- *The Future Results of British Rule in India* (1853) written with Engels
- *A Contribution to a Critique of Political Economy* (1859)
- *Herr Vogt* (1860)
- *Value, Price and Profit* (1865, first published 1898)
- *Capital Vol. 1: The Process of Production of Capital* (1867)
- *The Civil War in France* (1871)
- *Critique of the Gotha Program* (1875)
- *Capital Vol. 2: The Process of Circulation of Capital* (published in 1885)
- *Capital Vol. 3: The Process of Capitalist Production as a Whole* (published in 1894)
- *Theories of Surplus Value (Capital Vol. 4)*

Friedrich Engels

- *Outlines of a Critique of Political Economy* (1844)
- *The Condition of the Working Class in England* (1845)
- *The Peasant War in Germany* (1850)
- *Revolution and Counterrevolution in Germany* (1851–52, published in 1896)
- *The Housing Question* (1872)
- *Anti-Dühring. Herr Eugen Dühring's Revolution in Science* (1877)
- *Socialism: Utopian and Scientific* (1880)
- *Dialectics of Nature* (1883)
- *Origin of the Family, Private Property and the State* (1884)
- *On Social Relations in Russia* (1885)
- *Ludwig Feuerbach and the End of Classical German Philosophy* (1886)
- *The Peasant Question in France and Germany* (1894)
- *On Marx's Capital* (first published in 1936)

Also from Ocean Press

SELF-PORTRAIT
A Photographic and Literary Memoir
Ernesto Che Guevara

Self-Portrait, an intimate look at the man behind the icon, is a remarkable photographic and literary memoir that draws on the rich seam of diaries, letters, poems, journalism and short stories Che Guevara left behind him in Cuba.

ISBN 978-1-876175-82-5 *(Also available in Spanish ISBN 978-1-876175-89-4)*

CHE
A Memoir by Fidel Castro
Edited by David Deutschmann

Fidel Castro writes with great candor and emotion about a historic revolutionary partnership that changed the face of Cuba and Latin America, vividly portraying Che—the man, the revolutionary, and the intellectual—and revealing much about his own inimitable determination and character.

This edition includes Fidel's speech on the return of Che's remains to Cuba 30 years after his assassination in Bolivia in 1967, and provides a frank assessment of the Bolivian mission.

ISBN 978-1-920888-25-1 *(Also available in Spanish ISBN 978-1-921235-02-3)*

THE MOTORCYCLE DIARIES
Notes on a Latin American Journey
Ernesto Che Guevara, Preface by Aleida Guevara

The book of the movie, featuring exclusive, previously unpublished photos taken by the 23-year-old Ernesto on his journey across Latin America, and a tender preface by Aleida Guevara that offers an insightful perspective on her father—the man and the icon.

ISBN 978-1-876175-70-2 *(Also available in Spanish ISBN 978-1-920888-11-4)*

Che classics from Ocean Press

GUERRILLA WARFARE
Authorized and Corrected Edition
Ernesto Che Guevara, Preface by Harry "Pombo" Villegas

A best-selling classic for decades, this is Che Guevara's own incisive analysis of the Cuban revolution—a text studied by his admirers and adversaries alike. It's an account of what happened in Cuba and why, explaining how a small dedicated group grew in strength with the support of the Cuban people, overcoming their limitations to defeat a dictator's army.

ISBN 978-1-920888-28-2 *(Also available in Spanish ISBN 978-1-920888-29-9)*

THE BOLIVIAN DIARY
Authorized Edition
Ernesto Che Guevara

Che Guevara's famous last diary, found in his backpack when he was captured by the Bolivian Army in October 1967. It became an instant international bestseller. Newly revised, this is the definitive, authorized edition of the diary, which after his death catapulted Che to iconic status throughout the world.

ISBN 978-1-920888-24-4 *(Also available in Spanish ISBN 978-1-920888-30-5)*

REMINISCENCES OF THE CUBAN REVOLUTIONARY WAR
Authorized Edition
Ernesto Che Guevara

From 1956 to 1959, the people of Cuba struggled against immense odds to emerge victorious from years of brutal dictatorship, poverty and corruption. This is Che's classic account of the popular war that transformed a nation, as well as Che himself—from troop doctor to world-famous revolutionary.

Steven Soderbergh and Benicio del Toro's new films about Che Guevara concentrate on the episodes of Che's life described in this book and in his later journal, *The Bolivian Diary*.

ISBN 978-1-920888-33-6 *(Also available in Spanish ISBN 978-1-920888-36-7)*

Also from Ocean Press

CHE GUEVARA READER
Writings on Politics and Revolution
Edited by David Deutschmann

This comprehensive, best-selling anthology is the most complete selection of Che Guevara's writings, letters and speeches available in English.

ISBN 978-1-876175-69-6 *(Also available in Spanish ISBN 978-1-876175-93-1)*

MANIFESTO
Three Classic Essays on How to Change the World
Che Guevara, Rosa Luxemburg, Karl Marx and Friedrich Engels

"If you are curious and open to the life around you, if you are troubled as to why, how and by whom political power is held and used... if your curiosity and openness drive you toward wishing to 'do something,' you already have much in common with the writers of the essays in this book." —Adrienne Rich (preface)

ISBN 978-1-876175-98-6 *(Also available in Spanish ISBN 978-1-920888-13-8)*

FIDEL CASTRO READER
Edited by David Deutschmann and Deborah Shnookal

The voice of one of the 20th century's most controversial political figures—and most outstanding orators—is captured in this unique selection of Castro's key speeches over 50 years.

Fidel Castro has been an articulate and incisive—if controversial—political thinker and leader, who has outlasted 10 hostile US presidents. With the wave of change now sweeping the continent, this book sheds light on Latin America's past as well as its future.

ISBN 978-1-920888-88-6 *(Also available in Spanish ISBN 978-1-921438-01-1)*

oceanpress

e-mail info@oceanbooks.com.au
www.oceanbooks.com.au